An Egg for Lunch

Written by
Jill Atkins

Illustrated by
Leo Trinidad

Lin was at the farm with her dad.

"Dad," she said. "Can I have an egg for my lunch?"

"Yes," said Dad. "But you must get it from Pen the hen."

Lin ran to the chicken coop.

She met Pen the hen.

"Pen," she said. "Can I have an egg? I need it for my lunch."

"Yes," said Pen. "But you must get a dish of corn for me. Then you can have an egg."

Lin ran to the barn.

She met her mum.

"Mum," she said. "Can I have a dish of corn for Pen? Then I can have an egg for my lunch."

"Yes," said Mum. "But you must get me a cup of milk. Then you can have corn for Pen."

Lin ran to the cow shed.

She met Cass, the cow.

"Cass," she said. "Can I have a cup of milk for Mum? Then I can have corn for Pen the hen. And then I can have an egg for lunch."

"Yes," said Cass.
"You can have milk."

"Thank you," said Lin.

Lin ran to the barn with the milk.

"Now you can have the corn for Pen," said Mum.

Lin ran to the chicken coop with the corn.

"Thank you," said Pen.

She laid a big brown egg for Lin.

Now Lin can have an egg for her lunch!